Epigrams on Asylum Walls

Table of Contents

Foreward..5
A Brief Memory/*Piles of Ends*..6/7
Lines Across the Pond..8
Circle Never Complete/*As Above So Below*..10/11
Three Haiku..12
An Informal Nonconstruction of Things Not Worth Reciting...................................13
Fo' Li Po/*Solstice*..15/16
Grenzkostenkrieg..17
Daylight Vigil/The Fisher King..18
The Wreckage of the Summer...18
Begging the Question/*Hero*..21/22
Compass...23
Mystical Accident 24
Wartide Sonnet/*Found Matter*..25/26
Sunday Setting...27
On the Critical Methodologies of Ancient Sardinia...28
Taking the Racism Out of Lovecraft...29
Prayer to SE/*Processional*..30/31
A Lesson in Chaos/*Dolphin Overland*..32/33
A Toast to Eliot..34
Saying Grace/*Furtive Touch*...35/36
The Core of the Matter..37
Art/*The Haughty Courtier*..38
Cleaning the Canon...39
Back to the Beginning/Moment of Zen/*Spill*...40/41
Ruminations on a Rorschach Blot..42
Preyer..43
Pleasuring Oneself at School..44
Forever Forward/Chalk-art/*Light on Clouds*...45/46
Poetics, Contra-Aristotle/*Alone Against the Prairie*..47/48
On the Different Tribes of Artist/Bathing Haiku...49
Deceleration Injury/*South of Heaven (Before the Burned Wood)*....................50/52
Gift Giving...53
Interruption..54
Two Haiku/*Shoreline and Ruins/Erosion*...55/56
Decisions Decisions Decisions...57
Newsflesh..58
Acting Among Divinity..59
I Dervish/The Ninth/*Anvil at Sunset*..60/61
Polyphemos' Complaint...62
An Anti-Epistemological Interpretation of Generally Manifested Phenomena.......63

Hallucinare	64
In Memoriam/*Towards Buddha Rock*	65/66
Destroying Careers	67
Returning to the Trees	68
Knowing the Score/*Strata and Shade*	69/70
Stultification	71
Counseling	72
Daily Lesson/*Narcissus*	73/74
Three Haiku/Public Case/*Through the Cold Gates*	75/76
Highway at Dusk	77
When you pray enter into your closet	78
Reflections in Cigar Smoke/*Ancient Dance*	80/81
John Walker Challenged Me to a Duel	82
Thanatopsis/*Rod and Mask*	83/84
Dutch Elm Disease is a Geographical Misnomer/*Hidden Channels*	85/86
Image/*Treelike Fragments/The Goat*	87/88/89
Epigrams (I-XIII)	90
Vibrant Roadside	96
It Will Take You Away	99
Clearly Seeing Through	103
Refutation of Zeno/*Lips and Deritrus*	104
A Local Myth/*Passing Water*	105/106
Field Creature	107
Postscript	
ManIFeast	109
Manifesto of the Apocalypse/*Stone Tears*	112/114

Foreword

You hold in your hands the shattered remains of a decade of writing, pieces scribbled and sutured together and cast out into the world with little care but to say, 'There, it is.'

These pieces have been culled from various notebooks, napkins, and cracked shutters to purge myself of this body of work, which has hung overhead for too long without the load falling or me finding a more comfortable position. With this selection, it can finally be set adrift while I go roving for new conquests and foolhardy adventures. Since the market for poetry lies in the most nefarious fringes of the world, I have assumed complete control over its production and will run through the streets tossing them out, so they may fall where they may. No one makes a living with poetry.

The photographs are meant as a complement to the text, a physical view of similar conditions in which the poems were produced, though varying greatly in time and situation. They are in no way connected with specific poems and the order of appearance within this book is based purely on aesthetic sense.

The prose pieces on either end are simple fables—one very old, one very recent—capturing certain aspects of artistic temperament more obscure in the poetry. The postscript contains the two dadaterror manifestos, written at the beginning and end of 2011 and first published on the eponymous blog. They may clarify some of my aesthetic principles or that may show signs of serious instability or pretense, which is high treason. Nevertheless, they are in the postscript.

Meaning, equipment, and processing are all unimportant here, only that some impression is made. If the impression is overwhelmingly negative, then it has been effective—likewise if something makes you weep, dance, or masturbate. The greatest effect I can think of is that you stop reading right away and rush off to do something new. The what, why, and how become discombobulated hieroglyphs so long as the action flows from that torrent of strong wine endlessly streaming around you, only asking for an upturned hand to receive and the other spill down across the earth. If you can drink like this, then even the banal will shine forth new. If not, turn the TV on again.

A Brief Memory

(recollected in the presence of ghosts)

As a young man, in far more distant days, I often wandered lazily through the decrepit streets of my hometown with no particular destination—not that it was possible to find a true destination here. Such walks sometimes helped to clear my mind, sometimes to stimulate it. The houses I passed were generally forgettable, as indeed, I have forgotten everything about them—or maybe vague impressions of run-down wood, peeling paint, front porches with broken and rotten steps still clatter in my mind from this time.

One day, just beginning my meandering as the sun began to fade, I decided to walk headlong into the dying light when I noticed a lone woman standing adjacent to me at the street corner. These streets the tryings of time and city life scarred brutally, a ragged amalgamation of concrete and tar on which I trod endlessly and she stood unmoving. Nothing appeared terribly special about her at first glance, nothing eye-catching about her body, yet I had no desire to look away. What truly held my gaze was her long red dress: it seemed to rival the tiring sun in its trenchant color. I made my way over to her almost unwillingly, having nothing in my mind, romantic or otherwise, but, before I realized a pattering sound as my own footfalls on the pavement, I stood in front of her, calmly saying,

'Excuse me, but where did you get such a breathtaking red dress?' I nervously hoped my sanity hid the past few automatic moments well enough.

She smiled softly, not seeming surprised, 'Why do you ask?'

'I was struck by its brilliant color.' I said, 'I can't recall ever seeing such a glowing fabric. I'd take it for the sunset if I didn't know better.' We both chuckled. She seemed amused; I just tried to keep my embarrassment at bay.

'Well,' hiding her blushing at my innocent question, 'it has been in my family for ages, I am not sure of its origin. When my grandmother died she left me all kinds of unique little antiques.'

'Thank you. I didn't mean to pry if I bothered you. I can't believe I even came over here. I'm not exactly used to striking up conversations with perfect strangers, especially over clothes.' I blushed slightly now, but there seemed a rapport between us and the initial awkwardness smoothed into good humor.

'It's no problem. You made my day,' she smiled, brighter this time. 'I've been waiting here for what feels like forever. A date was supposed to meet me here hours ago.'

'I'm sorry. I hate waiting. But I hope you have a wonderful time tonight in some way or another. But now,' I continued as she began to open her mouth, 'I should be heading home. Thank you for humoring me.'

'In such a little talk? Never, it really was my pleasure.' She extended her hand, which I pressed gently, noting nothing special about her skin.

'Well, goodbye then,' I said after a pause, taking a step back, this system becoming more irregular and uncomfortable again.

'Goodbye,' she chimed, as pleasant as ever.

I turned, walking back the way I came, the sound of my footsteps exceptionally loud, masking any steps she might have made in another direction. I halted because the delightful stranger's voice called once again.

'My name is Elizabeth, by the way,' was all I heard, my back still turned away from her.

'I'm—' I began, however, looking back, all I gazed upon were the solemn rays of the setting sun, the exact color of Elizabeth's dress.

Piles of Ends

Lines Across the Pond (at Ft. Sill National Cemetery)

These white bones on the shore which lie like cancer
Of a distant great country shrouded in fog
And cheap goods and perfumes imaginations
Past never secreted. These grey-white bones
And freshly-mown grass drying brown shake,
And the sound of cannonade to the east,
towards the cross-timbers.
The cannonade fading against old bark
And sapling green; the freshly-mown
Grass drying in cannonade's sound,
The boom and bust and metallic echo.
The mown grass drying against the sand;
Into the sand the moans of generation
Spent and still barely that organic echo
Sighs and swooshes like the cloud-laden wind
Reaching through stone and tree—the shells.
Blue herons gargle hoarse songs, choking
On lacunae burned of powder and tobacco,
Holes from eagle feathers and heavy-dragging
Footsteps to the shore of a distant great
Country, populated of white bones and cool,
Lapping water like the sound of a forgotten flag.

Circle Never Complete

Her back curves like light bent
To reveal its every hidden shade
Through the prism of my sheets.
The sun cuts an obtuse swath
Into my pseudo-hallway, my open room,
Peering through my parents windows,
Spying on me as I sneak around,
Not wanting to wake anyone.
Aftershocks of our prom-night
Kegger registered on Richter scales
From San Bernardino to Java,
Yet I am the first one arisen.
For a moment, I want to climb back
To those immaculately sloping peaks,
Their valleys and outcroppings,
To survey my lovely kingdom:
The acres of trees felled for my library,
The fossils crushed and fermented
So that I may hear the dead sing,
The volatile fumes I conjure or stumble
Into: miasmas smelling of rotten juniper.
A blueness stretches from heart to beard,
And look, all my kingdom watered
With blood: my morning glories drop
Grenades of blood-stained seeds.
Aztec priests take them by the handful,
Watching the sun with me and waiting
For the sky-god to match his course
With their coursing veins—then
Thousands lose their bloody seed.
Weeping would blaspheme, and I
No longer laugh as I tread on the cross
Or gleefully piss on idols—in fact, I,
In this narrow beam, can feel no
Difference between myself and sideways

Rights that infinitely overstep their value.

I have ceased to distinguish dreams and realms.
Nietzsche tutored me in such overcoming;
Campbell in correspondence;
Woolf taught me how to jump,
even when weighed down, and
Pynchon, once I found him, not to seek.
After class I make a habit of killing teachers;
I learned more watching a half-full
Glass of milk shatter into the Big Rip,
And in short…I was a little cold.
Listening to Bartok, I heard strings unravel
Because we tried to understand why B-flat
Should follow an F-sharp minor chord;
Shakespeare turned to Greek once I pulled
Apart Titus' anger or Bottom's folly.
Hearing about private prisons, rationalism,
Anthropomorphic gods arising out of animism,
About closed linear systems and tangential functions
Tumbles into hurricane and my serotonin-enforced
House I don't think will stand much more.
Hearing moans and fingernails tearing flesh,
Hearing whimpers and uncontrolled wails,
Hearing lectures and due-dates, wages,
Prospects, mortgage rates, my body beginning
To creak more and more everyday—
I abdicate this land: heavy lies the crown.

Only now, with that widening beam,
I watch her back arch slightly—each inspire—
And pay no heed to everything's expiration.

As
Above
So
Below

Blossom Haiku

Single yellow rose
Stretches of the sun's smile
Drops of utmost woe

Haiku for Cinco de Mayo

Wine's red flowering—
Deep silent gasp after the
Universe's birth.

Haiku for Eric

Watching blackbird flocks
Cachinnate as Dolphy flauts—
The sun is setting.

An Informal Non-Construction of Things Not Worth Reciting

Egyptians sipped on lily-laced wine
To put the memory of eternal rot
Into an opiate-clouded corner and…

Trail the trial and whip Christ with
All the passion out on the streets
Of London soaked in whisky and Ire
toothless

Sequence-less—and see the sea harden…

with coffeespoons I stir the purple quintessence
of lucid dreams and smoke the limbs
of generally godless apes and Aesir;
break into—;
fabulous disintegration between
Buddha and proton and electron sits sidelined
And never neutral enough.

This thought has damned my whole generation
because air is sinful and this air throws keys
from the Divine Mr. Dolphy's keyless anti-swing—

dead at before forty,
dead at twenty-seven is more numerologically satisfying.

See the sea harden and soften,
See the air undulate and thicken,
See the earth slip into something less comfortable,
See fire spring from laughing Listerine bottles.

Wormwood! Wormwood!
Hamlet's oedipal synesthesia lies laced
with menstrual-blood-red notes,
words collapse into the Sphinx and uplift

Mahavira riding naked on a throne of young girls
And barbecue ribs dripping down his inner skins…

Can't you see?
If I could define something anew I would
obliterate lexicographer and return to Lascaux.
Oh—
You can see

Everything
Wove like DMT into Bufo chromosomes
until dawn comes to show us a bundle of
disorganized meat—an infant uncalculated
like a towel pulled strand for strand by an infant.

Were anything to come together
I would lose the joy of different books—

Since I can do anything
I'm at a loss…

Let him who hath understanding
end without hesitation
and never speak of trying or learning why
Lorenz made the weather out of butterflies.

Let him who hath understanding
lie about a day spent cross
Sinai whipped quicksand and dervishing devils:
Lawrence made his own name whether.

Let me approach my king
This brush loaded with three days of dead hair:

regicide is only a clearing of the brush

Fo' Li Po

Over a bent cedar, the moon sets
As the sun rises; the moon sets
Like a broken mirror slowly
Falling through the air above a trash-heap.

The wind blows down the moon
And I shiver, feeling more at home
In moonlit hallucinations than
Among academics and pandering students.

Let me walk the space between
The stars, and bypass the heat
And violence; let me have silence
For a moment, and the winter wind.

In silence I hear the slight dusting
Of departing butterflies, the soft
Rain darkening dirt, touching in concrete
A memory of its brief initial state.

With a sip of red wine I drink
The scars the moon won't show—
Its true face descending behind
The cedar bent for reasons I cannot fathom.

Solstice

Grenzkostenkrieg

Strike up the crescendo, begin the requiem:
No rest, play until strings break, lips blister,
And reeds mold—art is only a mirror to life.
Play to the bullets' tune, that whistle heard
Too late, or play nothing—anything will fail
To capture that last breath, the soul uncaptured.

We, we the people, weep over numbers and
Pretend the family's grief is no different than
Our momentary sobriety—who was lost yesterday?
How many of us have trimmed one thing out
Of our Wal-Mart list? Half the country might
Have gone hungry to fight Germany.

This time we can't even arm the army,
And sell it to ex-Seals turned profiteers;
Rome trained the Goths in shield-walls and
Short-swords until Alaric's alarums blew down
Marble gods and mottled senators—do I see
A correspondence? No, it can't be—but
America's water supply has steadily blackened
Since we learned how to wage war without
Imperative, or even declarative sentence.
The sentence passes too quickly and the subject
Lost; bin Laden slipped underground again.

A Hummer with a Dubya sticker passes on my right;
Hot copper nails slice a Hummer, sticking into the
Right side of a William or—some W-name—
His tag too scorched to read, and he cannot say
Who he is, or, soon, who he was, in the field
With berserker armor and flagging spirit.

Daylight Vigil

Miles above, clouds, not more than wisps, float
Indifferently to bustling Beneath. In strong strides
They ride as gods, our holy spirits forsaken on
Far, craggy shores of seas feared and haunted.
Millennia past, new superstitions smoothed our
Minds, smoother now than a child's, bading us
Forget how to cross these waters, bading us fear
Dubious monsters prophets once howled into
Dithyrambic terrors—once we had instincts to
March over them in mocking stride, now vestigial.
Here, in untamable heavens, ride Odin and Sleipnir,
Hunting heroes to people the glittering hall.
Ethereal valkyries gather those few seers left;
Their soft skin warms forgotten hearts, raising
Spirits long impotent and infertile—a comfort
That disappears before my eyes as the spacious
Cirrus blow apart in icy astral winds.

The Fisher-King

Dewy beads hide in air on invisible strings,
Mirroring grey skies, blankets covering our
Common past: massacres manifesting destiny,
Plagues shrugged off with a cough, every
Soldier's family who watched a flag fold
At their door, an old man's last words
Denied even his own hearing—all these lie
Tangled in aerial strands, stretched between
Cedar wall and cracking bark of a nameless tree.
Humid air hums apathetically; in its canopy,
A spider rocks back and forth without moving,
Calm as the tears framed on its carefully styled hair.

The Wreckage of the Summer
(a surreal memoir)

At last the last lifeboats leave
And yet a few of us remain on deck
Waiting—as the sun rises we shall
Be bloated on the freezing ocean.

It seems only yesterday taunts echoed in my ears:
Drunken peasants carousing, bragging, swaggering with nothing else
that carries them out of their station than cheap intoxication.
Between drinks we told stories of invasions: days when scant valuables shoddily walled in our homes were
ripped away and we lived in fear that things could only get worse.

Isn't that why we boarded?

Looking back as port's careful structuring gave way to ocean's mayhem
We cheered and embraced: finally, finally, distance between us and them.

The sturdy hull of *Summer* we did creak in dances
Vivacious and utterly wild; goddamn our god-man
Traditions, this moment's swirl of skirts and sweat
Shows me as much as I saw in wide-eyed adoration,
Those anxious moments when walls breathe prophecy,
When light, bright of its own will, obscured night
And day and the stars belly-breathed into grey pencilpoints.

Arising to the smell of scurvy and failing food,
Dive back into drink—you goddamned dogs!
Save me a pitcher: I feel mange's inch as well as you,
I encouraged you to join me, to change your situation,
I was encouraged with your company, the realization
That this ship and its isolation carried us specifically;
We had to see how far we could travel together.

I watched your eyes tighten as god left and could not say a word.

Still we stayed together, gathering what we could of memory, crying over relics in the dust—crying at the dust moved, ignoring gaudy icons—a small alliance, but for some short time it was ours as the *Summer* swelled in storm-winds and blistered when the wind died and the ocean stretched out, a vast glass desert and we had no means with which to further on.

And then we ended in the scheming North,
Icebergs rolling past: I sigh at the splendor,
Next to me, two laugh full-mouthed,
Yellowing the frozen pages—I sigh
At the splendor.
Later we traded complements, Blooming closer
than we imagined on first meeting.
Often we had nothing to say, nothing new,
Nothing interesting, but there existed
Understanding somewhere behind the silence.
At least, I thought so once—with things
Now floating past I'm not so sure.

What is this crumbling sound I hear so loud?
Night always brings terror, but to this end we came calmly.
There are plenty of lifeboats, people, abandoning ship
Will be easy—those who stay with me will pace tensely
As the water laps our feet and we wave off others trying
To pull us overboard.
I have not heard the word 'other' until now.

Distance grows,
And between you and I and you and her and her and I and her and whoever else
It grew until there was no depth in silence,
Until it became the steel door slammed
Between us.

Every man for himself.

Our ship drags down many captains.
But sitting here, you and I talk solemnly
About the empty cans rocking against

The boards, sounding like off-rhythm
Echoes of those dances slipping away
In our bluing flesh and in repressed
Thoughts that we left in the lifeboats.

Sigh with me, sir, but do not shiver,
It is beneath us both.

Begging the Question

What is enlightenment?
Image you are Atlas
Who must hold the world
Then remember
Such things impossible.

Hero

Compass

Today our souls come as items in a catalog,
The catalogs arriving right after Halloween
And flooding continuously until Christmas.
Mine a compass, each direction marked with
Sacred Indian totem—at least, I read they were
Sacred totems, lacking wisdom to judge otherwise.
Everyone seeks in life the symbol suiting the
Soul best, the one percolating that incomparable
Sense of home no matter what hell devours you.
Ordering it from the god on the line—surprisingly
Easy to telephone and very courteous, despite
Tall-tales of vengeance and narrow paths—
I waited at the window, hoping with everyone
Else that each passing brown truck contained
That precious soul-mark, the tangible soul itself.
My box arrived, like all others, right on time;
Every pour tingled, my head warmed as blood
Flowed with unknown vigor—on the verge
Of my guiding spirit, just a cardboard lid away.
The container—a wisp of air in weight—opened,
Revealing only cotton padding, the precaution:
Such things are notoriously fragile.

Mystical Accident (First Glimpse of God)

A young child, laughing, caught in some fantasy
Game of chase—perhaps running from T-rex—
Bolts upstairs in grandma's house to escape.
Turning the corner, worn orange shag, hideous,
Pads his swift feet passing through bedroom door;
From the wall, a vision stops the innocent boy
Dead in his tracks—eyes stare, mouth gasps agape.
In lacquered black walnut: a man carved in agony,
Blood rolls from slashes in his brow and he looks
To heaven as if help, someone to descend and save
Him, has forgotten this unknown innocent man.
The boy falls to floor, the bed a wall, keeping out
The image which causes more fear than scolding,
Doctor-visits, or a dark house devoid of parents.
Quietly, worried a slight sound may rouse from
His wooden tomb this man eternally enameled,
The boy crawls out of grandma's bedroom with
Its dusty, undisturbed smell and out of the tortured
Man's pleading eyes—not a word ever repeated,
He will never find true words to speak of it.

Wartide Sonnet

Dead feet have shortly stepped over this troubled ground;
Shuddering earth, turned mud through humanity's rain,
Is beset with twisted spires of wood, iron grain
That yields poisonous fruits and deafening silent sounds.
Black clouds—caustic, decadent—hide eternal points
Which, though always changing shape through ticking time,
Still chant their primordial suffocating rhyme:
Lungs, fill with boiling blood; come death, now anoint.
Now fields balefully blossom out of soulless steel
Vines we still entwine, not itself to grow 'neath wheel,
Beacon since first life raised fists to sky in wonder,
But to reap those caught in its thorns: the beastly meal.
   Through battlefield vineyards harvest hymns sing in groans:
   Come new seeds, come new storms, let new crops be sown.

Found Matter

Sunday Setting

Simple lines for an anniversary
We were so close to missing, a year
So many paranoid creatures posted-up
As the Never-To-Be-Reached,
The summit of human futility
Desperately crowned with zero,
Buddha's smile we have never
Not been dancing underneath.
Yet we entered as tritely as
Conjunctions thrown off without thinking,
A mere stumble from course to class,
Past to future, subject to predicate,
Master to slave and all such stereotype
Dualities that absorb minds so infinitely
More than the simple, singular burp
That supplies all corporeal coordination
And Whose-Lack ends the world
Of man and perhaps after there is
Less solipsism, less reaching
With arms of flame and shrapnel,
Less capitalization of signs common to all.
Lines here again demarcate
The birth of two saints whose worlds
Lie in eccentric orbits and do not revolve
For they needed no other side.
Yet they appear as different
As black and white, as martyr and matron
Filling out her ninth decade of quiet
Devotion to the same cause without
Speeches or marches or even eloquence,
Just warm pots on New Years like this,
Gumbo and rice that kept filling bowls,
And always someone willing to make room.

On the Critical Methodologies of Ancient Sardinia

From centuries of mutilated trees there grows
Those ignoble words ringing our judgment
On morality, psychology, mythology, and trembling life,
However, as soon as lips they have left close
Silence brings their end save dim echoes
Signifying nothing and not understood.
Every fact can be counter-proven given
Proper stances, flexibility, thought taut
Enough to systematically warp steady states.
But no steadiness can be relayed, whether
Political, economic, physick, atmospheric,
All become imappropraitely tumescent
Or wither to a useless, mocked bobbin,
Given butterfly farts and surfeited fucks
Or backdoor shut to quick or not quick enough.
Trying to hold the lines together is sure
Method to collapse, to madness, to hate
Of self, other, non-other, not either, and all—
But, awash in internal vibrations pure,
Hysterical gossip drowns in sensation
Freed from ideas about his sin or her filth,
Taints, sodomy and bondage and dripping.
Reflection, stripped bare and tied,
With albeit soft cord, but unable to hide
From the little dying pangs of this moment
Now this one and now this next, yes!
With zeal like Russian conscripts they fall
Into humid depths evolved to keep us safe
And sound yet throbbing and streaming
And casting brother's blood onto the ground.
The Voice does not comes to ask where
He stood and why now he is hidden—
The grasp ripples over the universe
With clear signs that need not be grasped
Or defined or delimited, only experienced,

Heard like static, and, once ended, need no resurrection
To say things further that never needed
Saying, moving as unchaigned as unheeded.

Taking the Racism out of Lovecraft

The most terrifying thing, I think,
Is watching clouds blow past,
And the people under them not
Seeing that the world, too,
Is blowing away.

Prayer to SE

Human hearts throb in a distant half-time round,
Lubb-dupp, an academian's only playful coinage—
I cannot hear it that way.

Hindus hear breath as a cyclical two-four sound,
So-ham, an exacting drone, bellows of every sage—
I cannot feel it that way.

Hebrews read the holy of holies in parallel time,
YH-VH, forgotten ululations, palimpsested lines—
I cannot know it that way.

I know one word only—the metronome of every heart,
Timpani-rolling of lungs, most scandalous pseudonym
Of any anonymous highest—quantumly echoing through
Chambers and stops, manifesting my mind and those
Of my dim allusions above,

Subsuming dank sputters of speech's artifice and mind's
Premature electrical ejaculations gumming up the works;
Rhythmic motif recurs as sleepy adagio for strings: S.E.

Processional

A Lesson in Chaos

Stepping out to piss, October sun thrusts
Into me, an overcoat two sizes too small.
A cloud of black specks stirs air mad with heat;
Gnats into my glowing hair, sticking like sequins.

Shake, adjust, zip; wipe brow, dissipate cloud;
Walk on. This private park, my playground,
Extends verdant hands to meet mine as long
Companions, hands of knotted, supplely stretching,

New growth and bag-worm-buboed branches—
Bodies fragrant, searing, envenoming, visionary.
Brown flutters, like sun-burned autumn hair ready
To fall to earth—butterflies whorl in Mandelbrot ballets,
Music by John Cage, updating that Kosma standard
Once all the rage, for one recital, presently.

Rice-paper wings kiss me: final fermatas, double-bars;
Rice-paper wings shut each land's proselytizing mouths;
Restless wings, scuttling cyclones greater than Katrina.

Dolphin Over Land

A Toast to Eliot

Dust is the most compassionate thing in nature,
Claiming no comparison of stronger or weaker;
Bellowing no blame if trampled, kicked, shat-on,
Noticing nothing of the sort; remaining still if stirred.

Men fear someday it and them will become one:
An anonymity more than most can lift without
Simon's shoulders, but the gentle dust threatens
No force nor blinding glare of promise unchained.

It exacts no taxes, no price for protection, as it can
Offer no protection. Dust, throughout vast nights
And utmost space consuming dead starlight, might ask
To be humanity's blanket, hiding us from cruel April.

Saying Grace

Thanksgiving day—eve more accurate—the light
A warm blanket now wearing threadbare; memory,
Old coats shredded as rags for dishes or genitalia.
'Everybody get ready to say grace,' auntie says,
Not with authority, though no one objects; hope flits
In her voice, but mechanism overrides her movements,
Overrides prepubescent memories of clasp hands.
Grandma begins slowly, nearing ninety, "Lord, bless us,"
Choking back tears for empty chairs, a husband and
Youngest child. Her words quaver and fade and the
Clock's obsessively sways before our gathered eyes.
How many still believe words make a difference?
Do I, who cannot even bow my head as her prayer
Plays on, "and this bounty spread before us.
In the name of Jesus Christ, our lord, amen."
Mumbles of amen slip out in hushed tones,
Grunted for appearance of piety, relics collected
Never far off, though I think my aunt spoke
An earnest "so be it." Indeed, I can agree
With those words, they reach more deeply than
Others; at least, I see them in themselves and
Simultaneously insuperable—suffice to say, I see them.

Amen.
Let sunlight fade and leave us cold.
Amen.
Let these people, my kin, fade away.
Amen.
Let our food be consumed and leave us famished.
Amen.
Let our star dim and blacken as it must.
Amen.
Let all stars dim and blacken as they shall.
Amen.
Let all energy slowly reach nirvana.

Amen.
Let all dissolve into silence beyond conception

Furtive Touch

The Core of the Matter

'We need inspiration before we write,' I say slowly,
Removing her headphones, her book, her inhibitions,
Penetrating her mouth like the scent of strong coffee
On whisky-sore mornings, tongues dashing and stirring
Sacred spices in our textbook milk-and-honey sacrifice.
No, we dance distant from Zion, from Jordan's bloody
Bubbling tides, twisting into caverns far removed from
Spent soil and lewd terrain; the shrubs' craggy reaches,
Trees' arthritic fingers, pine eagerly for our attention
To falter: facing mirror-polished obsidian, they wither.

Skins are peeled back, outgrown and itchy, hanging as
Ghostly fragments, energy without potential, useless.
Sudden as death, all and one collapse, blown-out like
Elaborate candles drowned in breathy sea-breezes;
Thought recedes below subconscious, below instinct,
Ever-constant DNA couples grow loose and rakish.
All gods wail, starve, and softly fade to ash of ashes,
But our wings faintly trail off, melting as we touch
The summit, as we imbibe solar fire and scatter
Supernova across our dance-floor, our bodies.

This whole time, our fat black cat
Lay asleep on the new futon.

Art

As I feel

As I write

As I feel the
Writing ripping
From my hands

                Like grenade shrapnel
                Like air in Auschwitz

The wind outside
Wraps the house
So powerfully
My desk shakes

           The expanding gases
           In both mind and world

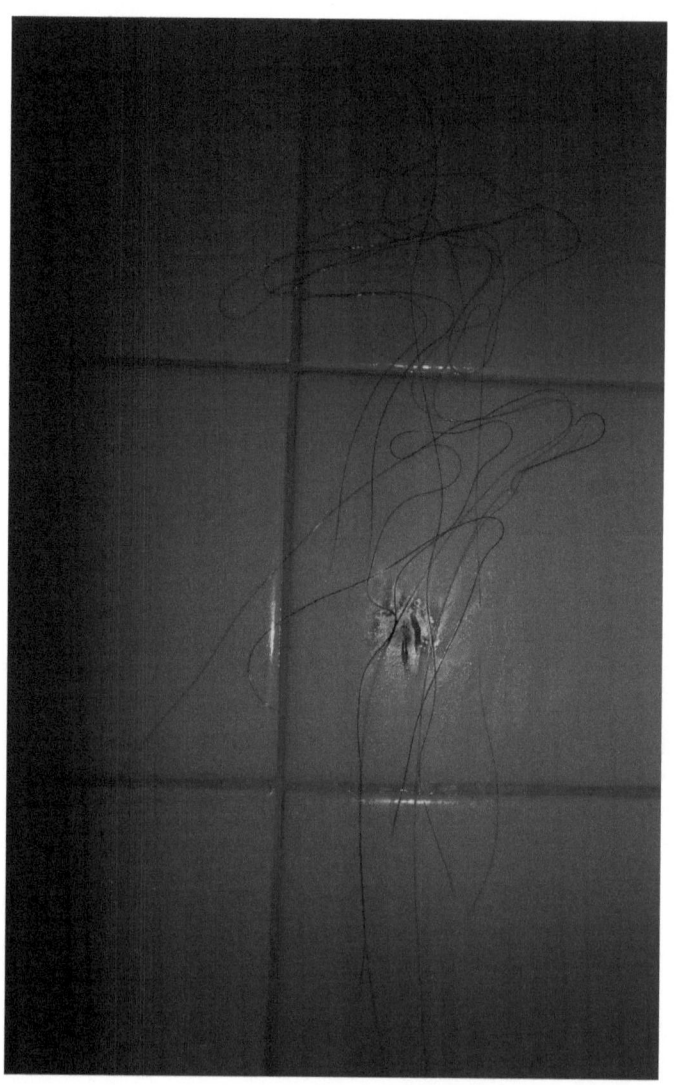

The Haughty Courtier

Cleaning the Canon

Shakespeare taught me love and loss and wit;
Donne schooled in ways weave the fabric finer;
From Byron I learned to stand, fight, and not sit;
From Blake, wars within awakening mystic seer.
Emily and Emerson revealed the revealed word
In every leaf and twig covering autumnal earth,
Leaving Whitman to uncover forms unheard.

Baudelaire crafted staggering decadent artistry,
Wine and women's every drop worth a library;
Rimbaud wrought still more ethereal scents,
And from the Comte—ennui's came-and-went.
Rilke drew Void's grinning mirror into pauses
Of breath's inhalation; Eliot exuded it from
Pedestrians' senseless, ever-subordinate clauses.

Ezra was left foundling history's fragments
In a brown paper bag from speakeasy nearest;
Poor, tortured Sylvia brought ominous depth
To conchshells exposed as salty tides relent.
Collins betrothed present-days to egregiously
Aged style; but, the ultimate lesson came from
Bukowski: don't take anything too fucking seriously.

Back to the Beginning

I want to touch the world as it was,
Before footprints ravaged maiden soil,
Before plantlife dared change chemistry
Of yielding dirt, absorbing and emitting
Vulgarities of nitrogen and oxygen.

I want to see this place as barren rock,
When breath came only from violent collision,
Renegade debris launching interstellar terrorism.

I want, if only a blink, a whiff, a twig's snap,
A world beyond symbols and analytical criteria,
Where a cross, inverted or not, equals absurd coincidence.

Moment of Zen

Sometimes, when I pass people
In the mall, in line at Borders
Or Barnes and Noble, a man fat
Or bald or old or any combination
Of those will be staring intensely
At me when I catch him out of the
Corner of my eye, not obviously.
He always seems offended at my
Long hair braided perfectly, my
Ring not a simple wedding band,
My quiet humming of old standards.
Whenever I see him, greasy grey
Shirt and jeans stained with oil,
Bad beer, and frustrated time lost,
I have one quiet wish: to walk
Slowly his direction, smiling and
Blindside him in the jaw—crack!
Fucking bastard.

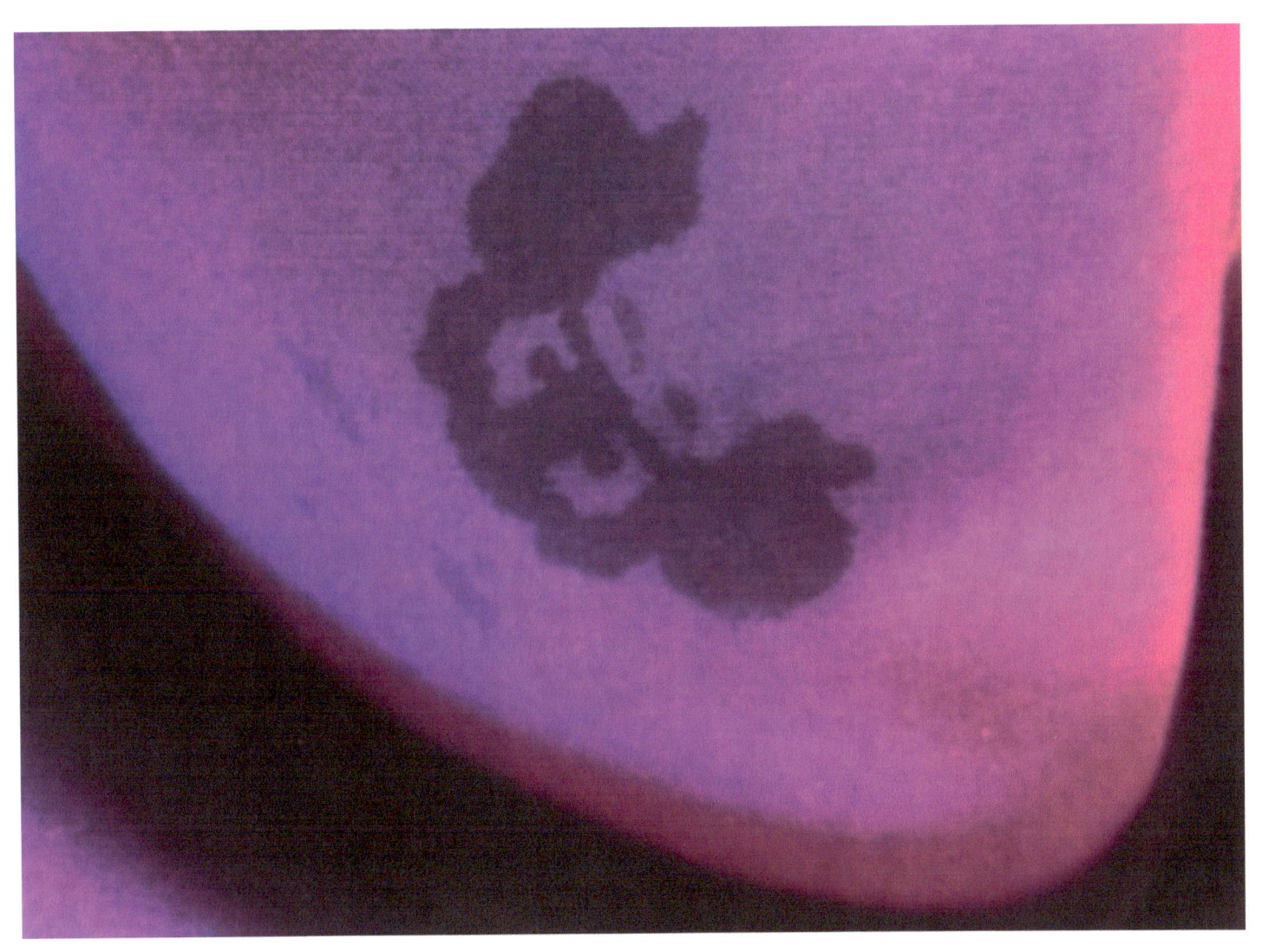

Spill

Ruminations on a Rorschach Blot

I see man
Not *a* man
But everyone
All traits living breathing sucking feeding
Male and female amalgamated shoddily
This new Christ, son of man,
Hideous leprous beyond repair and alone
On this planet
Kneeling on water

He is not wet
No drop slips the seems
Tattered grime-hardened rags
No moist secretion embraces
Fibers in pure sex (Shakti)
No

He sees his twin
Like a memory, a dream
Warped and vague
Over-stretching
Soundwaves casting ceaselessly over
Miles of highway traffic
Crying babies awaiting mother's tips
Knowing she absconded long ago

World in a ripple
He drowns
Floating on a sheet of air
Just above
Cool undisturbed
Water

Preyer

As over grey tombstone neverending I speed
Down I-44 East—though heading northeast—
And next to the roadway lies perfectly restful
A former raccoon: mint condition roadkill.
If blood did not frame the bandit's body
It would seem asleep, no sign of that lost
Spark in mother's empty eyes that evening.
I wonder from where the animals come,
Never spotting them alive while driving, them
Never checking left and right before scurrying,
And I pay more attention to grass edging
Its cruel garter than to the concrete piss-trail,
Crammed into the same line with different metaphors.
What does a raccoon or armadillo think
Crossing here—does the humanity's dominion
Smell different, do their feet feel artifice?
Is it to them simply more rock?
As for a truck who cannot stop—who callously
Cares not to—is there any difference in those
Last few synaptic arcs, or just that one last
Predator who proved too agile, too swift?

Pleasuring Oneself at School

The tiles are beige.
Softer colors supposedly soften
Temperaments, and who needs
More pacification than a tired,
Largely disaffected youth—but
The tiles glare despondent
In their lifeless chill of beige,
And they soften nothing of
My throbbing urge.

Whiteness stains the windows.
Paint splashed haphazardly
Decades ago and never retouched,
Patterning the adjacent tiles
Like some goth-kid suicide
In the high school bathroom—
One way someone would notice.

Humid breath condensates on glass.
Thick flows the atmosphere;
Windows, so caked in grime
Vision becomes negligible,
Become sticky in the tepid air,
Cannot keep a diseased breeze
From blowing on my t-shirt.
Standing in my dark corner,
Reading Ellison's <u>Invisible Man</u>,
Percocet faintly rubs my shoulders,
Turned towards the door
To pretend nothing's happening
If perchance intruded upon.

Forever Forward (The Road)

Celtic knotwork binds life in art.
Not some masterpiece of learning
Encompassing all experience (sorry James),
But a blanket for each person,
Carried atop bloody, worn-out
Wool shirts, an intrinsic reaction
To phenomena and external stimuli.
Lattice under the surface: religious embrace,
Governmental care, wise counsel,
A rope-ladder reaching to purest love.
Warm and inescapably beautiful,
Yet in its loops lie knotted
The doors of perception (sorry William).
Without Alexander's soul we lack the infinite.

Chalk-art

Three artists, three friends of mine,
Drawing on the parking lot
Of USAO's tiny campus,
For an art and academic contest.
Two pose, playing tic-tac-toe, while
The third outlines their shadows,
Gently white on the April-hot asphalt—
Wind-swept atom-bomb photographs
Slowly slipping towards forgetfulness
In Hiroshima's rubble, 61 years before.

Light on Clouds

Poetics, Contra-Aristotle

A poem, I am taught in school by
Respected and disrespected teachers
Alike, should be a word-picture,
An image captured photographically
In English's unsteady pixels.
However, Oklahoma bears little worth
Capturing: green grass sprouting amidst
Brown blades, from drought-whipped earth
Like the budding black pubic hair of a
Thirteen-year-old girl in our perverse jokes,
Or scenes of that same girl's face as the
Over-driven school-bus, its over-driven
Driver on over-driven, roads drops her
A block or two from her house.
She walks past a black man cursed
Publically by a white woman;
Dogs careen into chicken-wire
And slaver lustily at her; entering
Her door, she greets her mother in
Cracked pleather reclining amid empty
Doritos bags and an apple missing a few bites
Turning the chair's shade of brown—
Her mother's rolls of fat mirroring folds
Of her beloved throne; daddy will be late,
If he comes back at all; her brother runs
Around in usual five-year-old fashion
(can't blame him).

This girl, eyes like fading grass outside,
Procrastinates past homework, bee-lining
To the bathroom after her mother's wave
Of greeting and dismissal.
Leaning against the beige door, barely thick
Enough to dull the dysfunctional throb,
She sighs and locks herself securely away.

A razor offers pain, but in less than two minutes
She's smiling, though she can no longer feel her muscles.

Alone Against the Prairie

Of the Different Tribes of Artist

Writers are surely the most bothersome artists—
When they accept the title and don't decline
With Caesar's smile—and in comparison to comrades,
The most schizophrenically unstable, whether in
Parisian salon, English coffeehouse, or vernal Christiania.
A musician—classically trained—becomes at worst
A pretentious bell-ringer, and a rock star, just a drunk,
Junkie, or psychotic (when Morrison = Cain/Christ).
Painters (by implication every graphic artist) may be
Drunk or depressive, a prude often and well-equipped
With arrogance—though at their most monstrous, only
Melodramatic and ridiculous. But the writer—whether
Novelist, poet, playwright, scholar or philosopher—
Can be drunk, junkie, psychotic, neurotic, melodramatic,
Hypochondriac, depressive, prude, and bastard, and
Those simply reveal a lack of passion in the work.
A virtuoso cherishes music, a painter, sculptor, etc.
Loves the brushes' smooth glide and canvas's metamorphosis.
However, a writer views pen as pain in a thin case,
A needle caked in heroin and blood, screaming for use
To stave off sickness, and use only leads to greater need.
This special mentality leads other artists to set writers
Apart and call on them only in greatest need or general boredom.

Bathing Haiku

Three good ideas came
In the bath; I sneezed; only
Remembering two.

Deceleration Injury

The pews are padded rather nicely, but
Orange upholstery? Why would a funeral
Home use orange upholstery in its chapel?
Not a holy color, nor particularly happy.
Dimming sunlight on Indian paintbrushes.

We are gathered here today for Grandma Morgan.
Actually I am here to support my lover:
It's her (step)-grandmother, whom I met
Only once—seemed nice, obviously ailing.
She slept in a van her grandson was driving
When a truck turned into them; the stop tore
Her abdominal aorta and she died without waking.
No one else was hurt in the packed van
Except for some bruises and glass-scrapes;
Driver sprained his left wrist, though he isn't
Even cast at present. Near the geographical
Center of North America: a pause, then this.

Her body was flown back to Oklahoma;
Survivors suffered another car-ride for days;
Those nowhere near seem more torn-up
Than those present; I am stoic.

As the pastor eulogizes typical Christian—
We'll see her again don't blame Jesus whom she is with in love and peace and light forever and ever for he is love and peace and light eternal and the way we arrive in the kingdom of god and the way she knew and someday we'll may know the peace she now knows if we invite Jesus into our hearts which I invite you to do now—
Someone's cellphone rings in the back.
We all ignore it though disgusted—typical.

Songs play equally typical abominations
Of desolation praising Him and missionaries
Selling to the disenfranchised help in His name

And not for common good—country Christian
Tunes with few chords and fewer insights—typical.

Pastor returns—
Before we bow our heads in prayer one last time I say to you if you are not where you should be with the Lord Jesus I invite you to do it now let us pray father god give Sylvia Morgan your servant the rest she deserves from leading a good life father god in your service father god and name and let her father god be at peace in the arms of your father god son the lord Jesus Christ we ask you this in all meekness father god and for your blessing father god on Sylvia's soul—
Typical, selling at our weakest moments,
Clever marketing, but why this repetition?
Insecurity, or maybe His attention wanders.

Filing out, I didn't know this was an open-casket
Service, forcing us to stare mankind's excessive
Morbidity in its ritualistic face, made-up and neat.
People laugh and socialize lobby-side before
Departing to the interment in her birthplace, Hess,
Unmapped nowhere twenty minutes south.

The procession moves either too slow—through
City traffic as spectacle—or too fast—over state
Highways trying to make good time—never at
A respectfully steady pace. However, we made it
To CRN207 and the bent signpost bearing marking:
Hess, no population, no information, only distance.

The cemetery—all apparent in Hess—took up a low
Hilltop: we look over level fields, no houses, no
Community, trees only at graveside to shade shades.
White stones leer, hard to read if legible at all.
Many children vanished here: 1906-07, 1909-09,
1912-12, aged 9 mos. 14 dys.
Nothing beyond 1973 except this last teardrop
Memorialized in this forgotten place, this hell
Roasting at one-hundred-five degrees Fahrenheit.
July is no time for melancholy.

May she rest in more peace than I see in this cruel place.

South of Heaven (Before the Burned Wood)

Gift-giving

My cat passes through his special door meowing—
His usual demurring eh—at first hearing, typical
Of his main talents: getting attention and refusing it.

Hearing him presently I am completely naked,
So is the girl next to me; petting a pussy would be
A nice way to relax, to wait for sweat to dry,
To feel the spirit resurgent, before I'm ready
Again.

I snap my fingers to call this fuzzy black beast
Over before looking for the first time, seeing
His mouth full and the tail dangling limply
Like a thick, dead whisker.

Jumping up to shoo him and his new toy outside
Only causes the killer to flee under the futon
While a different kitty's mouth is wiped clean
After a different kind of meal.

Standing in the doorway, limp and glistening,
My shadow pours onto the driveway, black
Semen spent and rejected, liver-blood oozing
From birdshot trails.

Under mattress shade, I see him, not eating, just
Watching his prey eek. Too large to be a mouse,
Irregularly twitching, a flashlight reveals to me
A baby bird.

Don't look, I say, moving to her on the cherrywood
Frame, the psychedelic mattress cover covering
The body politely—eyes now shut, beak slightly
Parted, as if snoring.

A paper-towel destined as its death-shroud, I
Wrap the soft, still-warm body. Outside the air
Is too muggy, windless. With a heave, the bird
Flies across the frontyard.

I am still standing naked.

Interruption

An ant was just crawling over a notebook page
Where I was writing some inconsequential thing.
Normally, a finger would descend, and, lifted up
Again, flick away the suddenly grotesque speck
With an adjacent digit—a fleck of dust unnoticed
Eternally, the dust-mites not withstanding.
Tonight, however, I stopped short of homicide,
Trying to direct the rust-colored creature with
The pen in my hand. Wherever the Cross pointed,
The ant turned, and, continuing to halt its progress—
God knows what scent drew it to blank college-rule—
It quickly learns the limits of my glorified dart:
Both used in games of accuracy, both wound
In small strikes though just where it hurts.
The ant's sheer speed begins to out-maneuver me,
Soon it hides in my favorite notebook's spinal spiral
And our chess-game has made a Murphy out of me,
Though this loss comes with fewer moves, less explanation.
Continuing the interrupted writing, this little Endon
Runs back out onto the page's heading, its only mark.
Now the index finger—that which guid'st the golden
Ink-scepter—descends directly, sending the supplicant
On a kinetic journey past the Al DiMeola CD
In front of the white Epson printer always unspeakably
Loud and slow: enough fucking around,
I'm trying to write something consequential.

Two Haiku

I
I read a Zen book
Wavy humid Easter air
And did not learn much.

Shoreline and Ruins

II
I saw a Zen text
Stiff from icy Christmas kiss
It; mind; fell away.

Erosion

Decisions Decisions Decisions

So much to keep up with,
                            so much.

So much to sort out:

      What is a hobby,
            What a passion
                   ,
             A calling
                  ?
                        What first?
Loving to write   but also to read
         To play guitar   and bass banjo clarinet tablas
      Practicing yoga and gung-fu
                        To learn   e x p a   n   d
What art to become an –ist of?

All artists have lovers
                                      But what is higher
                   Lover or artist   ?
                   What first?
A writer
         yet   incomplete incorrect
            grammar
                         Voices recount
             All is art all is poetry break rules

If art is everything then art is nothing because art loses any special meaning.
If god is everything then god is nothing because god loses any special meaning.

                        What first?
          All art then
      Mediocrity
                             Good for me
                                   so widespread

Any talent stretched to mediocrity

        What then

                      Should be

                                The most stunning mediocrity

        What art?

                What first?

Fuck life

                        says Watt.

Newsflesh

Look but don't touch.
Yes: look; stare; feast your eyes
On war-orphans; cry your
Sorrowless tears when another death
Broadcasts from the second Iraqi War.
Stare—as if something dwelt behind
Those eyes—at car-crashes,
Gang shootings, teenage suicides,
Drug-addled infants, Asian jungle plagues;
There are too many people to save
And even Jesus reaches his limits.
Watch Ethiopian famines and AIDs
Running through the sub-Sahara
Like its Olympians; watch cancer
Kill soccer-moms and kindergarteners;
Artists too poor, pop-stars too rich;
Riots over voting rights, judicial power,
And cartoons. Keep watching.

Acting Among Divinity

Since I have lived,
God has played every role:
His hands applauded
When I thought the
Spectators faceless.
His eyes glared as father
When I talked back;
His eyes welled as mother
When I ran off in fear
Of punishment.
He has been Caesar
And Brutus
And Aaron the Moor,
And I took what other parts
Were necessary
At whatever time:
I have stabbed
And been stabbed
And famished with him
Chest-deep in earth
Until the earth reclaimed.

I Dervish

Some days it seems I will tumble through the spaces
Between words on a page, each line cracked in false walls,
And I need only to pluck the right chords and fall into
Alternate realities where nothing has changed but book
Positions and obviously—to me, sole referent—
Clocks run slower, days shorter, night hotter, and light redder.

Obvious things exist smaller, just barely; I feel, just so
Vaguely, heavier, though I couldn't have gained weight,
For I still sit at my desk, writing, which always produces
The same unopened doors and broken strings—here,
Even light slows down and refuses to bend.

The Ninth

As no energy can be lost or gained,
Nothing ever can be risen above;
Those beatings, humiliations, failures
Forgotten though not overcome.
For something to be forgotten,
The brain pushing those shadows
Of tears and leather belts into some
Dark night of hippocampus or amygdale
Will never be enough;
Each lost memory will be absorbed
Into behavior and attitude, reaching instinct.
A German boy bleeding
Madly recites poetry through black bars,
Though the symphony for him is silent.

Anvil at Sunset

Polyphemos' Complaint

A spider crawls out of my mind's eye only
It is not my mind's eye but a burned scared
Charred socket where Nobhdy thrust a spike
White hot when once I stumbled too drunk
To know what the trickster planned though
I bet I would never have known the whole time
Drunk or sober even watching him plot and scheme
And now a spider tickles me as she slips out
To do this or that I'm sure she'll return with food
Probably with food why should I mind her mind
In my mind's eye we do not interfere with one
Another our unspoken agreement obviously
Unspoken as spiders cannot speak or know
Of such things as speech or language or utterance
But who's to say I understand everything certainly
I do not claim any unfathomable knowledge
Since I lost track on this polytheistic journey
If you have already left there is nothing left
For you and if you stay I make no promises only
That I will continue as I am forced to continue
For some force even compels the spider
With her black unshaven legs moving
So succinctly so calmly so perfectly determined
In her unspoken determinism she is
Such a follower of fate I know this much
I am though I would say I shouldn't be
So willingly I force it out and art is achieved
But art is form defined so I create anti-form
A counter to nature though my purpose tries
To show nature in more natural forms than art
And who's to know or judge or determine how
It is achieved alone on this burned out island
For in trying to abolish form I seek to abolish
Art but still try to capture something something
A bit more natural and even in that I must turn

To art which is what I try to abolish in losing
Form and art and now without my mind's eye
Truly nothing is accomplished and my father
Dead under the waves how can we survive
In art or without cause and natural things too
Must be possessed must gain abstract instinctual
Art known as thought and reason and intent known
Only to those already possessing it but the spider
Returns to my massacred forehead the cavity where
Should sit my mind's eye and she dots her period
Period.

An Anti-Epistemological Interpretation of Generally Manifested Phenomena

Two people walk down a street;
One turns at the next intersection
With a wave—no words.

Hallucinare

I look on every sight that can be sighted, and yet
Focus on nothing. I think I see cares, but they
Could be rabbits chasing foxes, who I am to say
Who pursues whom anymore; it could be the devil
With a hatchet and polka-dot pajama-pants.
My guitar untunes itself as soon as fingers slip
Over the frets: strings corrode into cobras and
Rattlesnakes tangling themselves in my hands,
Biting endlessly—their venom, no more effect
Than cool water, their jabs piercing unfelt.
Retinas lose focus voluntarily—how I see.
My eardrum's head too loose to transmit vibration,
Even static inaudible, the big bang's faint
Ever-present drone dissipates—claiming deafness
Would be dishonest though. Body hair dissolves
Into dead grass, sun-bleached, roots long-since
Broken away to sink deeper in earth's recess,
To find the spot just before coldness turns to fire.
New sprouts lie down, hanging on for no reason
I can tell; a dying soldier crawls from the trench
Of my ass reaching for a butterfly drifting down
In search of drying nectar, frankincense, myrrh;
Folly, as the plants all lay down, supplicants.
The soldier dies as his hand extends over
Leafy wings, falling, crushing the monarch
Before it could cross to friendlier borders.
My eyes have turned into wooden balls, toys
For drowned children; termites arrive quickly
Carrying off usable portions. Can I be said to see?
Books translate themselves into every language
I don't know, at least, they did this before I lost
My sight, shifting into unwritten isolates.
If I can still believe memory—though I know Mumir
Gone, shotgun blast, squawk, and faint rustling
Before my ears went flaccid—but what's recalled?

Where was I? It's all ry'lehian to me.
Sulci form rivers surging underground, desiccating
This body, what used to be called 'my body,'
Or it seemed once before churches erected themselves.
Skin turns into frail bark, falling away slowly
Piece by piece. The wind reduces outdoors to inside
And the inside falls further and further inwards.
A droplet drops before everything is blown away;
Landing, leaving a black stain on the dirt, covered
Over in the next gust: I arise naked and laughing.

In Memoriam

    Go ahead

Practice asanas in thousands
Face cave walls for nine years
Humming
Wu-wei wu-wei wu-wei
Dance in absurd circles
Spill wine over black earth
Accept all offerings equal

Shantih Shantih Shantih

But remember
Krishna's leactured
To carry his rider
To war against his family

Towards Buddha-Rock

Destroying Careers

The thing-in-itself is itself an absurdity.
From any philosophical standpoint,
Logic breaks down the second such
A phrase is uttered. A thing-in-itself
Would be just that thing: a rock, a coffee-pot,
A cheap microwave taking five minutes
To boil water. How can there be just a thing?
Everything breaks into smaller units;
Everything intelligible, an alloy of others
Generally more general and abstract.
Obsidian descends to molecules,
The molecules atoms, the atom sub-atomic
Particles, those particles, perhaps strings;
The coffee-pot, glass and plastic, standing
And sitting at once, somehow simultaneously
A ghost-white and mountainous sentry—it
Spews the shit of god while I invoke Grafendorf.

From the artistic pose, who would want
The thing-in-itself? Description impossible
And no one around to share the failure:
No pens, paper, typewriter, Microsoft Word,
Author non-extant, as the thing-in-itself
Realized ceases to be
In-itself.

Returning to the Trees

I thought I heard your wind-up bird today,
Mr. Murakami, as I turned the herb garden.
Once sage, lavender, tomatoes, asparagus,
Different mints, now dried up over heartbroken
Summers. A few asparagus still rise every year,
Springing phallic then a foot tall tomorrow.
Rosemary, loving drought, now a bush,
Dominating the barren patch once a garden.

I thought I hit a rock, but rocks don't chip
At a shovel-strike. I tried to dig it out,
But earth claimed more than my energy
To exume. Chunks breaking off this object
Like fragments of bone after years
In acidic soil, porous, almost orange.
'It's the peach tree stump,' she explained
How it used to bear fruit before sickening
And rotting away. I remembered, though
I did nothing but listen and dig.

The first tree I climbed; barely eight feet tall.
Once I fell to a branch slashing from
Intestines to the right nipple in a perfect
Diagonal. I cried at first. My parents told
Me I was fine; I agreed with silence when
Only the peroxide burn remained and the long
Superficial blood-trail held primal temptation.

I believe I heard the wind-up bird on both days.

Knowing the Score

A cardinal sat on music-staff telephone wires,
Warped, ultra-modern, yet easy to follow taken
Line by line—compare to Carter, the human
Vascular system, Carter's human vascular system.
In any case, he sat like an unconventional fermata,
Some extravagant oxymoron in nature's film-noir,
Focus to all conceivable geometries and fears,
The sinister man brushing too close in line.
His streetlamp clef, shining with the twilight
So much more pleasant than fluorescence.
Behind, his sky too dark a blue to be the sky;
Rain, if backdrop drifts south becoming cover
Or ceiling, depending on mood, just as my tub is
Now half-empty. Melody out-maneuvers memory.
The bird gone, the movement over though he
Continues after a female. A wholly new sheet
Of staves—I don't know where to begin.

Strata and Shade

Stultification

I watched crimson sheets breath
Until they darkened and the room
Swirled as if I'd had too much wine
(or god). This is no metaphor.
I lay with my head to the pillow
And didn't blink, watching sheets
Breath as I couldn't, until they faded
To darker blood like a pierced liver.
Five dead hairs stuck in bizarre
Distribution graphs on the flat beige
Wal-Mart cotton, two rectangles
Flecked with blue lint from other
Blankets. Pillows provide little use
Save to chart hair collected overnight,
So flat—I never took calculus or I
Would solve things more thoroughly.
Still, loops and waves of mineral
Thread catch my attention long
Enough to contemplate their non-meaning,
Leaving them to graph continuously
In the air before predicating another
Predictable pattern in trashcan bottom.
The sheets have died, but I breath again.

Counseling

We've just received word to keep
Mrs. Woolf away from the rocks,
They make her so unproductive,
So unlike her flowing formless phrases
This stationary submerging; such
A contradiction, her Parmenidean
Stasis in Heraclitus's gaping maw.
Perhaps she knew the irony when
Filling her coat and mounting the rail;
Perhaps such contradictions finally
Made her realize we're all going mad
Again; perhaps she only wanted
To preemptively prove Camus wrong,
Though proof remains unnecessary.
Fear no more, only despair and smile
At passers-by and old perverts, for
When everything can be understood
Speech will become impossible.
So I leave her with silicate implants,
That heaviness, somehow too human
And somehow always too far beyond
Most humans: a sideshow tent on fire.
Words tumbling wavelike through
Her calculus, precision infinitely fine,
Though of course imperfect as art
By definition. Maybe that holds
The most beauty: her equations'
Impeccably fine work shimmering
Cold as quantum mechanics;
Understanding perception's most
Intimate episodes continuous,
Yet still, that is, fixed to initial
Points of creation and recording.
Understanding can only find itself
In Otherness, as an application,

As a possibility, a negation.
So I keep Mrs. Woolf flowing along,
With rocks no longer a concern,
Following her faint fingers tracing
Dalloway's day, lighthouse beams,
Leonard and Vanessa's uncovered
Thighs, novels never germinated,
Still remaining myself here and now
Under spells she's always moaning
Under purple waves crumbling above her.

Daily Lessons

Vapor trails in parallel lines—
Two dots dragging false comet
Tails down determined paths
Ending with their pilots desire.

Vapor trails already blown away
—no pilot, no plane, no choice—

Narcissus

Three Haiku

I
Always unlasting,
The fire crests and ceases;
All ways unlasting.

II
A cedar branch snaps,
Tries to force a sneeze—I will
Suffer so it will not die alone.

III
My redwood Buddha
Collects dust in details too
Fine for me to clean.

Public Case

A monk asked the master how the dharma will be observed after the death of the universe. The master replied, 'we shall have to think about bigger coats.'

Through the Cold Gates

Highway at Dusk

The horizon, jagged-edged paper torn
Away at last cool dark against sunset,
Purple fading out to dense red,
Red filtering into endless water above.

Wisps, vapor stirred and settling,
Dusty grey, smelling of smoke.
How can I see the Wichitas' ripped
Fringe when it always rips further?

Today: eroded grit from the mountains
Rises wildly, condensing into clouds—
Eskimo-kisses in arid convection.

Suddenly, the sun sinks too far, the last
Span fell fast enough to see it disappear.
Then the afterglow, the cooling.

When You Pray Enter Into Your Closet

Shoveling through my closet, dust from packed shelves
I want to forget and cannot bear to cast away
swirls to life, crawling on mangled legs into my pores,
breaking down capillary walls, a slight tingle shifting
slowly into a burn—unforgettable, tolerable—subdermal.
Blood by osmosis turns viceless dust virulent,
bisecting blood-brain barrier with coroner meta-culousness;
melancholy mannafeasts before I exit into well-lit corners,
out of this annex, this buried bunker, this vestigial gland,
rummaging through diaries forged in the last silly war.

I do not remember these memories,
but, usual graphological variations aside:
this cow-colored Composition book is in my hand,
and this tiger-striped artifact with black spiral spine
like a diamonded rattlesnake.

My genuine hand-painted-by-the-poor-
indigenous-people-of-tiny-raped-ravaged-possessed-
obsessed-site-of-generations-of-smallpox-syphilis-tribal-war-
between-England-France-Holland-Belgium-Portugal-Germany…
didgeridoo huffs in the door's left-hand corner, unplayed;
saying Australian would have been too simple, untruthful,
especially as it comes from Indonesia.

My green onyx camel, lying down under a date-palm,
shapeless stretch of Yemen,
hand-carved by some fool in Pakistan.

Did he think his work would be appreciated?

Or the product of slave labor, carved to make a few
dollars for the boss and a few Americans feel cultured?

I will never meet who carved the simple, angular head.

Old toys on top shelf, less mounted
than balanced on the clothes bar:

half-painted steel, Tonka plow,
yellow and red, grey showing through;

a fire-truck,
white plastic ladders
easily stretching to
the highest floors of
burning desk-apartments
whenever I, as God, chose
them to ignite (amen)…

Melting into a dripping mass—breathing carcinogens—
old songs tossed in to blaze their greatest performance,
never to return to the repertoire.
Crackling, this initial glory a cedar branch
in Indian ritual exorcizing ghosts still dancing
after impalement on bayonet, phallus, and bullet-dug trails.

Reflections in Cigar Smoke

My lungs speak a demon into existence;
arms reach around me, tremendous jaws tear
the frail taffeta generally regarded as reality,
engulfing me—who reared it
from fire, fiber, and ash.

The malignant beast vanquished at
a new breath respiring not of fleshy organs,
arriving after thousands of miles—not
arriving, merely passing,
ten thousand miles more.

To name it god seems devilishly
naughty, yet nefarious nonsense holds
no more heresy than my meditation's
smoky visage mirroring
Maya's illusive games.

Conjured in my breath, I forgot
I am powerless knowing not his name.
Wind's undeserved compassion
Breaks tobacco taste into ethereal
syllables, divine, though not divinity.

Ancient Dance

John Walker Challenged Me to a Duel

Blended Scotch pours into a frozen tumbler,
I can't afford single malt; frost swimming
synchronicity, a school of shark-scared tuna,
but alcohol quickly scores its fill,
and I scour my meal as top predator.
Twilight offers me wine, but I know
he'll poison me; I watched him collect
dying purples from wounds of all who
died today; mainly in Iraq, Lebanon, and
America's repressed inner memories.
Looking at ambrosia I feel drunk already,
but memory flies somehow unaffected;
distillated aconite could explain this effect,
and numbness begins through my chest.
 The fragrance of your breasts—you
whose breasts only I know—wafts through
the air; gone years since yesterday.
No matter if this water gives life to Ene-sei
or Cache Creek; no matter the smoking clouds
threatening to push devil's winds earthwise,
I am still wrapped and wreathed in
 your small, passionate hands, the cinnamon
scent of your body, wet scents
permeating atmosphere from traces
still on my fingers and tongue.
I taste it in the whisky: life indeed,
blood and body granted to me;
I smell the variations of your fields
in every gasp of breeze; I feel you
in every blade of grass, for I am
the grass slowly drying this evening.
I hear you in every audible sound:
each orgasmic scream,
each pathetic whimper of a dying dog.

Thanatopsis

See someone die and we are upset,
not for the victim, but for ourselves
and those people we see in the act of
this other's dying. Our families, our
friends, selves, brothers-in-spirit, all
become tenfold more cherished because
for a few days at most we know that
our car could slip over the guardrail
the only difference being proximity.
It frightens more to think the highway
will crack skulls quickly, like a dropped
egg, than it is to think how much
work the worms must go through.
If the sanitation crew has to earn their
bread, then death is sanctified and we
showed the conquerers how strong a
resistance this tired Roman Empire can
put up before it dissolves into the
power of individual landlords.

I, though, think of the lost one
And the poor color chosen to match
the grey concrete, not in mourning
but wondering where he went to school.
What happened to those first people
the shy boy blushed at in kindergarten?
What Christmas present swelled gratitude
in him, the most joy or most comfort?
He may not have been Christian after all.
What did he think as the overpass quickly
became more highly elevated than his black
Cadillac and threw him from the windshield?
Who will continue waiting in increasing
annoyance or anxiety?

Rod and Mask

Dutch Elm Disease is a Geographical Misnomer

I am an elm-trunk, bark-stripped
in a broad yard. My brethren
crumbling rings still in memory,
relations vibrating between roots,
struggling for nutrients, fresh water.
The grass too turns to nothing more
than a dying god's whitened hair—
bald before long.

I am bald, all bark chipped away with
wind, lightning, young boys throwing knives,
venting pubescent urges finding no other outlet.
Storms took my branches once shading lovers
and vagrants, then the adolescents swarmed
on something weaker, the same way I
used to take nearest elm, ash, or alder's
share of earth, the same way mushrooms
sprout at my feet like nobles kowtowing.

Hidden Channels

Image

An ant carried a feather
along a sidewalk today.
Working at my elementary school,
begrudgingly volunteered by my
mother who has taught there for
years; at least I am getting paid.
The old auditorium stage
needed dismantling; I carried
fifty pounds of phlegm-hued velvet
curtains (of equivalent age) to the
dumpster; oblivious to my chores,
the red soldier marched alone
with elegant if not oversized
insignia—a grey down crest
streaked black three times,
middling sergeant I suppose.
This plume must be pulled
from Plutonian night's wing;
an act deserving Herculean praise,
no matter how little bureaucrats
Acknowledge it.

Treelike Fragments

The Goat

Epigrams

I

Calm   inarticulate
                directionless   winds
    rustle through
    constantly sighing trees;
                  standing,
g   r   o   w   i   n   g   ,
to be their own mausoleums
                            once
                            no more
                                          rings can be forged
        their leaves and boughs
                swagger
                      up and down
                            like a drunken death dance.
Winds strive to reach
                n   o   w   h   e   r   e
                            over the soil
                            the trees
                            embrace.

II

God's voice has roared
in echo since first words
babbled what shepherds,
wanderers, and tyrants alone
Heard in deserts and forests.

Describing these words' works,
only one way says in sooth what
a Gold-mounded Hessen
wished humanity to be:
the space once a clay pot's use.

Today (and yesterday; tomorrow)
the pot lies broken on a dusty floor;
space within remains unchanged,
though, boundaries undefined,
too much infinity infiltrates—

Purpose dissolves without.

III

S
      l
   i
p
p
        i
  n
          g
…
just one moment

into
    another

                pleading for peace

      a treaty with time
pluck out
      his tongue
                    and eyes
   …
      now
this
                          too
            is past
        .

IV

Am I a poet or a fool?
Is there much difference
between the two?

A poet's chromatic words
supposedly paint all things
he thinks others ought obtain
in a glass of wine, a sea-shell,
a dying beatnik, a handful of dust.

The fool emulates these glistening words,
a more harmonically schooled crow,
more melodically gifted, more natural;
a good fool always knows how to play
the Duke wearing his colored chords.

His fault is the poet's missing meaning.

V

Piles of spent time I have learned;
words, age upon age, provided
ten thousand of the finest meals
I have ever consumed, greedily
from inscribed wooden coffins.
Instead of tobacco, I breath
the smoke of funerary fires;
the fragrance of Dido's burning
heart better suits me than Armani,
or pretentious Calvin Kline musks.
Polynesian cannibals eat battle-dead
to gain prowess otherwise wasted;
I breath burning souls to gain pains
never inflicted on myself, timely
folded, awaiting appropriate festivals.
Each book acts independently,
one of the now-innumerable norns,
twisting fresh thread from my back,
convoluting my Gordian path.
Wheeling sun my clearest mirror
unbreakable, though not discussing
its ideas, burning ahead, myhead.
Seeming to lack anything better
this pilgrimage should be enough.
When we reach Jerusalem twilight will fall..

Vibrant Roadside

VI

Stars in themselves the entire world,
they are nothing to me!
Here, the place nowhere in particular,
and entwined in the matted
braid of nature's mean,
meaning: carbon chains,
peacock's meow, futilely
violent bees, kamikaze.
Snakes converse in darkness
and nothing is, there to here,
somehow they say everything.
Every word of breathing time
spreads like a wave breaking
on an imaginary shoreline;
here, in the space between
twitching, huffing stars.
Let us run endlessly among
cool and crisp wheat-fields,

so easily lost.

VII

My room cluttered with books and music
in piles and rows of accountant precision.
These specimens: their glories, failings,
ambitions transubstantiated into me.
All of it unnecessary

when I see my lover smile—
knowing she consents to that title
—or when I see my cat killing a bird,
knowing his rape likewise consented.

More wealth lies in the teeth of that black feline,
the burning eye of my coming feminine,
than in these relics encircling my mind.

VIII

    Totally at a loss…
        and waiting for my woman
      to come home.
  She's gone only days
  and already at a loss.

    I try and wait filling
      <u>The Empty Pages.</u>
    Trying to play the beats,
        Kerouac in Western Colorado,
          no tea to be found, even in Mexico.

  Last rotten wooden nickel
      and I don't carry change,
        no more wine to kill the cold's pain.

  But I'm being silly again…
    only a few days gone
      only a few more to go.

I guess I love her and by guess I mean know.

    One more thing is sure:
    I don't know what it is,
    but there must be something.

It
Will
Take
You
Away

IX

Though we may fret for conditions and dreams
preserved like crustaceans in formalin,
I should like to tell the moon that she
rolls over a rolling rock, a glowing clitoris
fossilized for research and analysis,
no other aesthetic purpose or pursuit.
My myriad specimens, my work of
Faustian years, topple from oaken and
ashen shelves; earth does not move:
shelves vomit their overdosed contents.
I worked tirelessly to procure them, all the
time tiring more and more, polishing items
I created and preserved: a life's work,
though not a life's goal—achieved nonetheless.
Each gleaming jar, each dream I made sure
remained stunted and static, for consistent
observation, now slips into cataclysmic air,
but no danger of death stirs my heart,
precautions so far prove effective.
As they tumble and shatter on the floor,
I watch unmovable and unmoved.

X

I watched a crow kill a sparrow today;
a stifled chirp left its beak as the crow's
black gavel came down without parole.

Today I heard my voice in the waves;
it rolled through the oxygen-rich seas,
reached my ears and I gave a stifled chirp.

XI

Is that the sun, easing into its hot bath beyond
the horizon, or the salvo of nuclear war with China?
I cannot see a bomber, not B-52, not Enola, not
any class of Mig, Mirage, or Lockheed monstrosity.
I cannot see the sun's face; who's to say Thor's
red beard is not glowing past the skyline?
I see seven trees about me Romanating;
my brother clothed in freshly turned earth
between prickly cedar and groping wisteria;
slender snakes wrap tongues around our legs.
Is it the roar of passing cars, or
our children squealing like animals?

XII

When muses burn fleshy works of marble statues;
when the dead sun reflects light of a flaming moon;
when wolfpacks leave the woods and forage cities;
then all will awake to perceive the doors cleansed—
or rather, to see nothing at all different,
because human sight cannot but be finite.

The divine: mowed grass raked into a pile.

XIII

I have felt more at home in houses
of termite-chewed wood than in marble halls
lined with paintings of prophets and patricians.

I have felt more lonely when laughing
among friends who know my deepest fear,
than alone, wondering what it is like to be Atlas.

Clearly Seeing Through

Refutation of Zeno

I dreamed I was speaking with Zeno in a forest. The greenery at times distracted me from the philosopher; he did not seem to notice, explaining in meticulous detail why movement is impossible, each word annunciated beyond the possibility of misunderstand-ing. Seeing a rabbit run from a bush behind the Greek, I drew my bow and fired an arrow into his heart.

Lips and Detritus

A Fragment in the Margins:
        Paint chips hold more truth than the annals of all life because they can have no meaning.

A Local Myth
(collected from a toothless old man stinking of moonshine)

When the world was young and there existed but a few families of mankind, a child lost his parents in a great flood, becoming the first Orphan. His mother's sister's family took in the boy, still so young and already showing signs of great strength and cunning. The family had a son of their own, younger than Orphan; he did not share his cousin's traits. Their son was known to laugh or weep impulsively while watching the sun set or the blue ocean of the sky fermenting wine-dark, spending his hours amongst the wheeling stars. If his parents rebuked him for such idleness, he would reply, 'you said I have accomplished nothing, but nothing remains to be done.' His parents could not understand his reasoning or his moods, wishing fervently that he would begin to follow Orphan's example, who showed dexterous skill.

The two boys argued and fought constantly; often the son would end up in tears though Orphan said he was only playing. At times, the son grew vengeful and tried to get Orphan into trouble with the elders, but something always made Orphan's turpitude pardonable. While Orphan continued to grow, he began to hunt game in the wilderness, his skills proven immediately. Other families soon heard of Orphan and spoke of how he would one day make a great warrior and leader despite the loss of his family. The son never developed Orphan's skills; on hunting trips he cracked twigs along the trail to warn the animals and ran from tree to tree listening to birdsong; when fishing he saw Orphan pierce minnows and worms with the hook but the son kissed them and set them free in the water. People laughed at the son and said he would waste his life roaming the forest and singing to the rivers, wandering in the mind.

One day, the son was once again on his favorite path, lined with long grass and large red flowers, tress magnificently tall and streams of fresh cold water rippling abundantly down from clouded mountain peaks. The son came upon a stranger groaning in agony. He told the son a snake had bit him and it was obvious to the son the stranger was dying, having seen elk and deer die under Orphan's aim. The son quickly went to find the Snake, who was sunning himself in a grike. 'Fine Snake, quiet and powerful, tell me what may be done to counter your venom,' the son said bowing. 'You approach me without fear,' grumbled the Snake, raising his head only slightly, 'but you have also shown me more respect than any other man. Find a purple flower with black berries, give three berries to whomever you seek to help and he will no longer worry.' 'Thank you, fine Snake, the quiet and powerful,' the son bowed again and rushed back to the stranger. He lay right beside a bush of pale purple flowers and glistening berries, black like an oily nightsky. The son picked three of the finest fruits and gave them to the stranger, telling him to eat. The stranger's eyes grew wide and soon he could stand. 'Bless you, bless you, son of the woods,' he exclaimed and ran away drunkenly towards unknown expanses.

The son never mentioned his encounter with the stranger or the parley with Snake, he simply sat quietly while Orphan boasted of his hunting today, taking time to mock the son's idle hours, reprimanding him for not even gathering the nuts and berries that women collect. The son smiled but remained silent. 'Tomorrow I will go to the next family and take my wife,' Orphan said. 'I wish you happy bonding,' the son said, his smile somehow different. 'I will not be going happily,' Orphan grew agitated, 'her family has refused me five times. Tomorrow I will go, and if they refuse again I will kill them and take her.' 'Orphan,' the son ceased smiling, 'do not attempt this, no good will come of it.' 'I don't want your advice. I know what I will do. As my brother you should support me,' Orphan said firmly. 'Orphan, my dearest brother, if you go, if you and I go, if you were to take our whole family, the end would still be the same: this endeavor can only bring ruin.' 'Already your parents grow old, and mine have long since ceased aging,' and with that Orphan left the house and the son wept.

The next morning, Orphan prepared for war on the neighboring family; the son appeared without weapons or alms, only his flesh. The two did not speak as they headed-out, the son slower than Orphan, fading further into the distance. At the house of the woman's family, Orphan again began his supplication and again was refused. Rising angrily, Orphan cast down the father, but before he could strike the killing blow, he himself was struck with a spear. Orphan staggered back but did not fall; hearing a sound like bubbling water behind him, he turned and saw the son lying on the ground, blood streaming from his eyes. 'Oh my brother,' Orphan cried, 'it was I who was struck.' Tears fell down Orphan's cheeks and onto the son's lifeless face. Orphan fell dead across him, and the wronged family, fearing some terrible magic or some god's wrath fled far into the north.

As the sun set that evening, the son arose alive and wept over the body of Orphan. Under the full moon, the son burned Orphan's body in a bed of cedar, drinking a wine brewed from morning glories, singing, dancing, and wailing until the sun rose again. At daybreak, the Son went into the wilderness, learning the gifts and secrets of all the lands, revealing them quietly to whatever needy person he happened upon.

On the brightest nights, he can still be heard singing amongst the cedar and ipomoea, laughing and weeping like waves cresting, until dawn.

Passing Water

Field Creature

Postscript

ManIFeast
(an humanist invective against humanity)

There was, some decent time ago, a movement that sought to squash further movement,

REGAIN STILLNESS

But that message was irrevocably lost among the masses who stated their opinions about squashing movements without realizing their cacophonous movement. Authorities became everyone with a dada and thus everyone swelled with an undeserved pride at this complete open leveling. They failed to see that their opinions were the lowest and least graceful of movements, though often the most moving. Chance was beaten for answers, but only allowed lines and squares to slip through its tears and fall--the conception of work rested in the individual mind, and still existed, at that.

Then the pope of Brittany cried out that this tomfoolery was not to be allowed anymore, a new and upright kingdom was going to restructure sanctity among the previous scraps and shits and genetic discharges. First, construct the trenches, wall off infinitely anything outside the realm, put previous texts to the torch, kill the musicians, operate panoptic.

The dynasty ended with him, who spent his declining years desperate to justify something of the land he created, now surrounded by enemies and outshined by sycophantic neighbors with less energy and ability.

Then STILLNESS, now, STILLNESS right now,

The popes have succumbed to the plague. Their tunelessness caused their bowels to rupture, caustic harmonics unnaturally produced. There is no resistance in the wind as it folds and flows in invisible turbulence as much as a stormy sea is visible not resisting the stormwind. The key to following this movement is not to think about its dogma or direction, not to establish definite directions, leaders and predicted followings. Parameters at best. No movement with the movement or even at all if possible--but ideals are nothing if not half-remembered dreams that in that betray their very definition.

This convoluted, uninteresting wordplay is not any movement, not beyond reality or of it, this paper is only some sloppy dance around what needs to be said if people would only open their eyes and think of not thinking. There is nothing here that Tzara did not oversay in Zurich, nothing not included in those few paragons of babble that opened poor Hugo's soul to a still heretical god, nothing that Cravan's last bubbles in the Caribbean did not slip into that god's sleeping ear.

There is nothing to more understand if you can only look around awake. If you can, if your breath burns these words onto the page and effaces them at each cycle, then there is nothing more to read, ever. But that's not to say it isn't interesting to do so at times. Whatever hits the senses like an injection of DMT, like the savage spasm of sex, like a bullet, is truth. Whatever hits the senses at all, is truth.

Disgust is essential. One must see with ubiquitous disgust the borders and walls that have allowed such a proliferation of countries, ethnicities, languages, sciences, and conceptions to fill the world with such an infinity of bullshit that no one can find suitable materials or sound space on which to build a foundation. If no one knew from choosing to not know, out of conscious rejection to boundedness, it would be the day of judgment, the second coming, and people would realize the lack of necessity in all this bickering. All foundations can be supported in the endless play of human signs still salvageable in the refuse of history. From whatever is useable, forge a weapon strong enough the crack open the head of the Other, make the sight see what's inside one eyegoneblack--to quote the Bygmyster himself--and what is transacted cannot be exceeded in merit or holiness.

Sadly even this disgust, even this most honest tender-hearted disgust with everything, still betrays bounded thinking, as does the choice of conscious rejection--these means still mean on language and within language, always intermediated through sign-functions and change. The ruth of history is to prove how quickly these structures burn and warp in the black-hole tension of time. The trick is

CONJURE STILLNESS

To find that flicker where all language dissolves into Joycean dreamisms, where conceptions bleed together on the battlefield that never hosted a fistfight, where discrete units become inconceivable in the infinite gradient, substantiated by experience but impossible to talk about everyday (revealed/revealing everyday), the slow loop covering every possible trajectory at certain unstable moments (read: movement is moot).

Everything is permitted that comes down like dice--thus Gethsemane and Golgotha. For Jesus so deeply breathed-in the world, he had to suffer greatest to show mankind that they are all present in the bread, with only Logos, Transfigured, every crumb accounting for every atom of the universe--that is why he kept with whores and lepers. His last human torments were no less valid for their terminal quality; his last words of forgive us lifetimes of inattention and unawareness, only briefly shown in that local bit of anti-progressivism. If the wider worlds could give up their ghosts the same way--Ghosts extending to any abstract system or comprehension--Then hell would finally deflower heaven, the doorway cleansed of its doors with dynamite.

and thence STILLNESS

Ripples and waves are unstoppable, so do not press your hand against the water trying to calm it with soft or hard words, let it beat against you and admire its effort. Or do struggle, be modern and in the dying glory of the West sun rage, Rage, RAge, RAGe, RAGE against the dying of the light, only be aware that this effort is yours alone as perceiver, constructed according to your idiosyncrasies (filled out according to family's, society's, and history's) and not translatable with any accuracy. Cross the rubicon and know that with every movement the die is cast. Changes are established, but how it will play out is up to each player in his solo (with certain conditions constraining according to taste). Absorb your surroundings like water, because there is no other choice; reflect them however you best reflect, just remember judgment compounds the elementary.

With honest discourse, there is no reason a physicist, a poet, a plumber, and a phenobarbital addict could not together speak as much truth as any sort of pharisee. Any discipline can converse with any other if only people could remember that undisciplined place before conversation was possible, the fundamental unities (read: limitations) of human experience which has allowed the playful fruiting of every human endeavor. The whole earth resonates on the same scale, even though it is tunable to this odd expanse of timbres and tones. Played completely open, one's fingers across the ground should be as intimate as any naked tremblings between lovers, and no touch between lovers should be less attuned.

MOVE STILLNESS.

We are the poets of revolutionary nothingness. To be amongst us one need not produce anything but life, an energetic bond between beings, slight ripples, a play of partials over an always-absent fundamental. We reject nothing that is created with honesty, though it may be contrary to personal taste. We may speak of the importance of intensity, of gesture, of insight dancing to the other shore and back; however, we are aware enough to shrug it all off to properly feel the breeze.

We seek the STILLNESS of cave walls.

Manifesto of the Apocalypse

It is time.

For?

No, it is time.

Time for what?

Time for time to slip away. Time times change and we equal a vast sea of inequality, when seconds and minutes are counted the same and accuracy is a best-guess before squeezing the trigger.

Is it time?

Time is not to blame. It is always-already present in understanding; understanding of present/presence is contingent on time; time is always-already the necessity of present understanding; understanding holds time as the ultimate contingency necessary for furthering itself.

Who has time for this?

No one. Such definitions have weighed the arms of the clock eternally down and they are faltering, soon to spill everything we've piled so callously over it. From the array splaying out in chaos before us, we may choose all the raw materials of facility, reflection, action, and whatever physical matter that remains graspable, in the array splayed out, from chaos, before us.

What to do with time then?

Fritter it away. Make fritters, raise chickens, pull weeds, scratch your ass, read Harry Potter, smoke weed, practice a thousand thousand little deaths in preparation for the real thing.

What to do at that time?

When?

At the time of death.

Every moment is a time of death for the living. Once that time is upon one, all temporal relations collapse into infinity, which is to say, a speck of insurmountable weight impossible to locate except through disparate effects on active bodies—to speak of it is blasphemy.

How so?

Speech relates to things arbitrarily and can never touch the moment when the breath fails. Speaking as if it can provide adequate description is no different than eating from the tree of knowledge of good and evil.

How so?

That taste cleaved the human palette irreparably, opening the yawning gap between the sounds of what is said and the idea that the intended object could actually be incased within it. Shame was hidden not because it was, but because the concept of nudity overcame the simple reality of human nakedness. All our intractably exposed conditions become intolerable once (we believe) they are enshrined in abstraction.

Why?

Why what?

Why do abstractions inevitably lead to intolerable realizations?

Because before realizing it we just lived it. Once a concept can be crystallized around some infrequent experiential data, then it ceases to accept contradictory information, or it develops additional constructs with which to handle them—special groups charged with delivering brutal einsatz.

How?

Necessary information is handled as a contingency; contingent data is treated as necessity.

What is the difference?

It is impossible to say outside of a given moment in a given set of circumstances, given history and idiosyncrazy.

Then why the differentiation?

Because the whole picture causes madness, suicide, or monkishness.

When?

The moment one sees the folly of forcing the endless stream of analog data into discrete digital boxes, that instant of realization where one understands fully just how limited human capacities are and that our original sin, the knowledge of good and evil, is nothing more than the creation of good and evil, the human arrogance in thinking we have rights to absolute judgment, or rights, or right and left.

Then what is this?

Sin.

And where is absolution?

In the quiet moments before the shot. In marching across flat desert miles because there is no other choice, not murmuring over past indiscretions or cruelties, but continuing with useless steps in no given direction.

Stone Tears

www.ingramcontent.com/pod-product-compliance
Lightning Source LLC
Chambersburg PA
CBHW042031150426
43200CB00002B/16